interchange

FIFTH EDITION

2 B

Workbook

Jack C. Richards
with Jonathan Hull and Susan Proctor

CAMBRIDGE
UNIVERSITY PRESS

CAMBRIDGE
UNIVERSITY PRESS

University Printing House, Cambridge CB2 8BS, United Kingdom

One Liberty Plaza, 20th Floor, New York, NY 10006, USA

477 Williamstown Road, Port Melbourne, VIC 3207, Australia

4843/24, 2nd Floor, Ansari Road, Daryaganj, Delhi – 110002, India

79 Anson Road, #06–04/06, Singapore 079906

Cambridge University Press is part of the University of Cambridge.

It furthers the University's mission by disseminating knowledge in the pursuit of education, learning and research at the highest international levels of excellence.

www.cambridge.org
Information on this title: www.cambridge.org/9781316622711

© Cambridge University Press 1998, 2017

First published 1998
Second edition 2005
Third edition 2013
20 19 18 17 16 15 14 13 12 11 10 9 8 7 6 5 4 3 2 1

Printed in Malaysia by Vivar Printing

A catalogue record for this publication is available from the British Library.

ISBN	9781316620236	Student's Book 2 with Online Self-Study
ISBN	9781316620250	Student's Book 2A with Online Self-Study
ISBN	9781316620328	Student's Book 2B with Online Self-Study
ISBN	9781316620342	Student's Book 2 with Online Self-Study and Online Workbook
ISBN	9781316620366	Student's Book 2A with Online Self-Study and Online Workbook
ISBN	9781316620373	Student's Book 2B with Online Self-Study and Online Workbook
ISBN	9781316622698	Workbook 2
ISBN	9781316622704	Workbook 2A
ISBN	9781316622711	Workbook 2B
ISBN	9781316622728	Teacher's Edition 2 with Complete Assessment Program
ISBN	9781316622285	Class Audio 2 CDs
ISBN	9781316623992	Full Contact 2 with Online Self-Study
ISBN	9781316624005	Full Contact 2A with Online Self-Study
ISBN	9781316624029	Full Contact 2B with Online Self-Study
ISBN	9781316622254	Presentation Plus 2

Additional resources for this publication at www.cambridge.org/interchange

Contents

Credits   iv

9   Only time will tell.   49

10   I like working with people.   55

11   It's really worth seeing!   61

12   It's a long story.   67

13   That's entertainment!   73

14   Now I get it!   79

15   I wouldn't have done that.   85

16   Making excuses   91

Credits

The authors and publishers acknowledge the following sources of copyright material and are grateful for the permissions granted. While every effort has been made, it has not always been possible to identify the sources of all the material used, or to trace all copyright holders. If any omissions are brought to our notice, we will be happy to include the appropriate acknowledgements on reprinting and in the next update to the digital edition, as applicable.

Key: B = Below, BL = Below Left, BR = Below Right, C = Centre, CL = Centre Left, CR = Centre Right, Ex = Exercise, L = Left, R = Right, T = Top, TL = Top Left, TR = Top Right.

Illustrations

337 Jon (KJA Artists): 4, 22; **417 Neal** (KJA Artists): 1, 16, 67, 84, 90; **Mark Duffin**: 39 (Victrola, telephone), 51; **Thomas Girard** (Good Illustration): 32, 87; **John Goodwin** (Eye Candy Illustration): 36, 94; **Gary Venn** (Lemonade Illustration Agency): 30, 64; **Quino Marin** (The Organisation): 79, 91; **Gavin Reece** (New Division): 85; **Paul Williams** (Sylvie Poggio Artists): 42.

Photos

Back cover (woman with whiteboard): Jenny Acheson/Stockbyte/GettyImages; Back cover (whiteboard): Nemida; Back cover (man using phone): Betsie Van Der Meer/Taxi/GettyImages; Back cover (woman smiling): PeopleImages.com/DigitalVision/GettyImages; Back cover (name tag): Tetra Images/GettyImages; Back cover (handshake): David Lees/Taxi/GettyImages; p. 2: JackF/iStock/Getty Images Plus/GettyImages; p. 3: Slaven Vlasic/Getty Images Entertainment/GettyImages; p. 5: Baar/ullstein bild/GettyImages; p. 6: Jetta Productions/Stone/GettyImages; p. 7 (TL): Vasilii Kosarev/EyeEm/GettyImages; p. 7 (TR): skynesher/E+/GettyImages; p. 7 (CL): Richard Newstead/Moment/GettyImages; p. 7 (CR): Scott Olson/Getty Images News/GettyImages; p. 7 (BL): Cultura RM Exclusive/Dan Dunkley/Cultura Exclusive/GettyImages; p. 7 (BR): ALAN SCHEIN/GettyImages; p. 8: Daniel Allan/Photodisc/GettyImages; p. 10 (cable railway): Anthony Collins/Photodisc/GettyImages; p. 10 (ferry): Michael Coyne/Lonely Planet Images/GettyImages; p. 10 (subway): GILLARDI Jacques/hemis.fr/GettyImages; p. 10 (tram): marco wong/Moment/GettyImages; p. 11: Jack Hollingsworth/Stockbyte/GettyImages; p. 12: Sven Hagolani/GettyImages; p. 13: Stewart Cohen/The Image Bank/GettyImages; p. 14 (CR): H. Armstrong Roberts/ClassicStock/Archive Photos/GettyImages; p. 14 (BR): Johner Images/Brand X Pictures/GettyImages; p. 17: Jake Fitzjones/Dorling Kindersley/GettyImages; p. 18 (TR): Goodluz/iStock/Getty Images Plus/GettyImages; p. 18 (CL): KingWu/iStock/Getty Images Plus/GettyImages; p. 18 (BR): Coprid/iStock/Getty Images Plus/GettyImages; p. 19: Ethan Daniels/WaterFrame/GettyImages; p. 20: Thinkstock/Stockbyte/GettyImages; p. 21 (BL): 4FR/iStock/Getty Images Plus/GettyImages; p. 21 (T): Bolot/E+/GettyImages; p. 21 (BR): Lise Metzger/The Image Bank/GettyImages; p. 22: Lartal/Photolibrary/GettyImages; p. 23: Tony Robins/Photolibrary/GettyImages; p. 24 (CR): Anthony Lee/OJO Images/GettyImages; p. 24 (BR): Steve Brown Photography/Photolibrary/GettyImages; p. 25: Xavier Arnau/Vetta/GettyImages; p. 27 (C): Leonardo Martins/Moment/GettyImages; p. 27 (T): Michele Falzone/AWL Images/GettyImages; p. 27 (B): Michele Falzone/AWL Images/GettyImages; p. 28: FRED DUFOUR/AFP/GettyImages; p. 29: Hero Images/GettyImages; p. 30 (L): Tomasz Konczuk/EyeEm/GettyImages; p. 30 (R): OcusFocus/iStock/Getty Images Plus/GettyImages; p. 31: John Howard/DigitalVision/GettyImages; p. 33 (R): Blend Images-KidStock/Brand X Pictures/GettyImages; p. 33 (L): Laoshi/E+/GettyImages; p. 34: Rich Legg/E+/GettyImages; p. 35: DreamPictures/Blend Images/GettyImages; p. 37 (Ex 1.2): altrendo images/GettyImages; p. 37 (Ex 1.2): Maximilian Stock Ltd./Oxford Scientific/GettyImages; p. 37 (Ex 1.3): Tony Cordoza/Photographer's Choice/GettyImages; p. 37 (Ex 1.4): Tetra Images/GettyImages; p. 37 (Ex 1.5): Peter Dazeley/Photographer's Choice/GettyImages; p. 38: VCG/Visual China Group/GettyImages; p. 39 (TL): Stock Montage/GettyImages; p. 39 (TR): Roberto Machado Noa/LightRocket/GettyImages; p. 39 (CR): Ivan Stevanovic/E+/GettyImages; p. 39 (BR): Justin Sullivan/Getty Images News/GettyImages; p. 41 (Ex 8.1): Westend61/GettyImages; p. 41 (Ex 8.2): Prykhodov/iStock/Getty Images Plus/GettyImages; p. 41 (Ex 8.3): Jeffrey Hamilton/Stockbyte/GettyImages; p. 41 (Ex 8.4): Paul Bradbury/Caiaimage/GettyImages; p. 41 (Ex 8.5): sputnikos/iStock/Getty Images Plus/GettyImages; p. 41 (Ex 8.6): Image Source/GettyImages; p. 43 (TR): Charles Ommanney/The Washington Post/GettyImages; p. 43 (BR): Tetra Images/GettyImages; p. 44 (Ex 1.2): altrendo images/GettyImages; p. 45 (Martin Luther): FPG/Hulton Archive/GettyImages; p. 45 (Valentine's Day): Dorling Kindersley/GettyImages; p. 45 (April Fools' Day): Wodicka/ullstein bild/GettyImages; p. 45 (Mother's Day): Ariel Skelley/Blend Images/GettyImages; p. 45 (Father's Day): Ariel Skelley/Blend Images/GettyImages; p. 45 (Independence Day): Tetra Images/GettyImages; p. 45 (Labor Day): Blend Images-Ronnie Kaufman/Larry Hirshowitz/Brand X Pictures/GettyImages; p. 45 (Thanksgiving): Paul Poplis/Photolibrary/GettyImages; p. 46 (TR): PeopleImages/DigitalVision/GettyImages; p. 46 (CR): Floresco Productions/OJO Images/GettyImages; p. 47 (Japan): Eriko Koga/Taxi Japan/GettyImages; p. 47 (Morocco): Hisham Ibrahim/Photographer's Choice/GettyImages; p. 47 (Scotland): Education Images/Universal Images Group/GettyImages; p. 47 (India): Jihan Abdalla/Blend Images/Universal Images Group/GettyImages; p. 48: RubberBall Productions/Brand X Pictures/GettyImages; p. 49: Dan Dalton/Caiaimage/GettyImages; p. 50 (Ex 3.1 photo 1): JTB Photo/Universal Images Group/GettyImages; p. 50 (Ex 3.1 photo 2): fST Images - Caspar Benson/Brand X Pictures/GettyImages; p. 50 (Ex 3.2 photo 1): Glow Images/GettyImages; p. 50 (Ex 3.2 photo 2): Jason Homa/Blend Images/GettyImages; p. 50 (Ex 3.3 photo 1): David Caudery/PC Format Magazine/GettyImages; p. 50 (Ex 3.3 photo 2): David Caudery/Apple Bookazine/GettyImages; p. 50 (Ex 3.4 photo 1): H. Armstrong Roberts/ClassicStock/GettyImages; p. 50 (Ex 3.4 photo 2): Sydney Roberts/DigitalVision/GettyImages; p. 50 (Ex 3.5 photo 1): Thomas Trutschel/Photothek/GettyImages; p. 50 (Ex 3.5 photo 2): Justin Sullivan/Getty Images News/GettyImages; p. 52: Westend61/GettyImages; p. 54: H. Armstrong Roberts/ClassicStock/Archive Photos/GettyImages; p. 55: JGI/Jamie Grill/Blend Images/GettyImages; p. 58 (Ex 7.1): Roberto Westbrook/Blend Images/GettyImages; p. 58 (Ex 7.2): Marc Romanelli/Blend Images/GettyImages; p. 58 (Ex 7.3): PeopleImages.com/DigitalVision/GettyImages; p. 58 (Ex 7.4): Rick Gomez/Blend Images/GettyImages; p. 58 (Ex 7.5): Ezra Bailey/Taxi/GettyImages; p. 59 (TR): Sam Diephuis/Blend Images/GettyImages; p. 59 (CR): Betsie Van Der Meer/Taxi/GettyImages; p. 60: JGI/Jamie Grill/Blend Images/GettyImages; p. 61: Arcaid/Universal Images Group/GettyImages; p. 62 (Ex 3.1): Matteo Colombo/Moment/GettyImages; p. 62 (Ex 3.2): Alan Copson/Photographer's Choice/GettyImages; p. 62 (Ex 3.3): John Lawson, Belhaven/Moment/GettyImages; p. 62 (Ex 3.4): De Agostini/W. Buss/De Agostini Picture Library/GettyImages; p. 62 (Ex 3.5): Avatarmin/Moment/GettyImages; p. 63 (CR): Oliver J Davis Photography/Moment/GettyImages; p. 63 (TR): kimrawicz/iStock/Getty Images Plus/GettyImages; p. 64: John Elk III/Lonely Planet Images/GettyImages; p. 65 (C): Christian Adams/Photographer's Choice/GettyImages; p. 65 (BR): Erika Satta/EyeEm/GettyImages; p. 66: Yongyuan Dai/Moment/GettyImages; p. 68 (Ex 4.1): Redrockschool/E+/GettyImages; p. 68 (Ex 4.2): Milenko Bokan/iStock/Getty Images Plus/GettyImages; p. 68 (Ex 4.3): Jetta Productions/Iconica/GettyImages; p. 68 (Ex 4.4): Deklofenak/iStock/Getty Images Plus/GettyImages; p. 69: Rick Diamond/WireImage/GettyImages; p. 70: Marc Romanelli/Blend Images/GettyImages; p. 71: PeopleImages/DigitalVision/GettyImages; p. 72: Jamie Grill/The Image Bank/GettyImages; p. 73: Kris Connor/Getty Images Entertainment/GettyImages; p. 74 (TR): Monica Schipper/FilmMagic/GettyImages; p. 74 (BR): fotoMonkee/E+/GettyImages; p. 75 (TR): Popperfoto/Moviepix/GettyImages; p. 75 (BR): Metro-Goldwyn-Mayer/Archive Photos/GettyImages; p. 76: Buyenlarge/Archive Photos/GettyImages; p. 77: Ernst Haas/Ernst Haas/GettyImages; p. 78: ©Lions Gate/Courtesy Everett Co/REX/Shutterstock; p. 80: Alan Copson/AWL Images/GettyImages; p. 82: Karl Johaentges/LOOK-foto/Look/GettyImages; p. 83 (T): YinYang/E+/GettyImages; p. 83 (Ex 7.1): Marcio Silva/iStock/Getty Images Plus/GettyImages; p. 83 (Ex 7.2): Gary D'Ercole/Stockbyte/GettyImages; p. 83 (Ex 7.3): Illiano/iStock/Getty Images Plus/GettyImages; p. 83 (Ex 7.4): Silvrshootr/iStock/Getty Images Plus/GettyImages; p. 83 (Ex 7.5): Danita Delimont/Gallo Images/GettyImages; p. 86: BrianAJackson/iStock/Getty Images Plus/GettyImages; p. 88: Monkey Business Images/Monkey Business/Getty Images Plus/GettyImages; p. 92: Sam Edwards/OJO Images/GettyImages; p. 93 (TL), p. 93 (BR): Simon Winnall/Iconica/GettyImages; p. 95: BananaStock/Getty Images Plus/GettyImages; p. 96: Sporrer/Rupp/Cultura/GettyImages.

9 Only time will tell.

1 Complete this passage with the verbs in the box. Use the past, present, or future tense.

☐ buy	☐ drive	☐ do	☐ leave	☐ sell
☐ change	☑ go	☐ have to	☐ sell	☐ use

In many countries nowadays, food shopping takes very little time. In the past, people _____ used to go _____ to a different shop for each type of item. For example, you _____ meat at a butcher's shop and fish at a fish market. A fruit market _____ fruits and vegetables. For dry goods, like rice or beans, you _____ go to grocery stores. Today, the supermarket or superstore _____ all these things. Once every week or two, people _____ in their cars to these huge stores to buy everything – not only food, but also clothes, electronic goods, furniture, and medicine. But in the future, the way we shop _____ again. Nowadays, people _____ a lot of their shopping online. Soon, maybe, no one _____ home to go shopping. Everyone _____ their computers to order everything online.

2 Choose the correct responses.

1. **A:** When did people travel by horse and carriage?

   B: _____

   • In the next few years. • About 100 years ago. • These days.

2. **A:** When might doctors find a cure for the flu?

   B: _____

   • Nowadays. • In the next 50 years. • A few years ago.

3. **A:** When did the first man go to the moon?

   B: _____

   • Sometime in the future. • Today. • About 50 years ago.

4. **A:** When is everyone going to buy everything online?

   B: _____

   • In the past. • Right now. • Soon.

3 Complete the sentences. Use the words given and ideas from the pictures.

1. These days, _people go to the beach for vacation._ (beach)
   In the future, _they might go to space for vacation._ (space)

2. In the past, _____ _____ (collect CDs)
   Nowadays, _____ _____ (listen to music online)

3. A few years ago, _____ _____ (desktop computers)
   Today, _____ _____ (tablets)

4. Fifty years ago, _____ _____ (business suits)
   These days, _____ _____ (casual clothes)

5. Nowadays, _____ _____ (drive their own cars)
   Sometime in the future, _____ _____ (cars that drive themselves)

4 Music is change

A Read the article. How did popular music change?

Music Is Change

Popular music has changed a lot in the last one hundred years in the United States. From jazz to rock to hip-hop, music is always moving forward.

Jazz music began to make its appearance about a century ago in the United States as a fusion of European and African musical forms that people could immediately identify as something very new. Musicians all over the world began to play jazz and to make important contributions from their own musical cultures. An example of this is bossa nova (new beat), which began to emerge in Brazil in the 1950s.

Jazz evolved into Swing in the 1930s and 1940s, with large orchestras playing music that people would dance to. The big bands of Count Basie, Duke Ellington, Benny Goodman, and Artie Shaw were very popular. However, the expense of maintaining large orchestras and changing tastes led to a quite different kind of popular music in the 1950s.

In the 1950s, the rock 'n' roll electric guitar began to replace the jazz horn. Bands with only a guitarist or two, a drummer, and a singer became popular. Of course, the most important singer of this music in the U.S. was Elvis Presley. Like jazz, rock 'n' roll inspired musicians from all over the world, such as the Beatles from England, to make some of the best and most popular songs.

In the 1970s, alternatives to rock 'n' roll began to appear. Three of the most important new sounds were disco, punk, and hip-hop. Disco was famous for the rich sound created by studio musicians and the flashy clothes of the dancers. Punk was a return to small bands that played their own instruments very loud and fast and criticized society in their songs. Hip-hop began as a way to use record players to make music for parties without the need for musicians playing traditional instruments.

Some people say that these musical forms are the "children" of jazz. In any case, they are now played throughout the world with each country contributing its own very particular sound.

B What about you? Answer these questions about your own country's music.

1. What kind of music do you think your grandparents listened to? Do you like this kind of music?

_____

2. Was rock 'n' roll important to your parents? Was there someone like Elvis Presley or the Beatles in your country? Who?

_____

3. What kind of popular music do you listen to? Is it influenced by any of the musical forms discussed in the article? Which ones?

_____

5 Choose the correct responses.

1. A: What if I get in shape this summer?

    B: _____

       • You might be able to come rock climbing with me.

       • You won't be able to come rock climbing with me.

2. A: What will happen if I stop exercising?

    B: _____

       • Well, you won't gain weight.

       • Well, you might gain weight.

3. A: What if I get a better job?

    B: _____

       • You won't be able to buy new clothes.

       • You'll be able to buy some new clothes.

4. A: What will happen if I don't get a summer job?

    B: _____

       • You'll probably have enough money for your school expenses.

       • You probably won't have enough money for your school expenses.

6 Verb pairs

A Which words go with which verbs? Complete the chart.

- ☐ a cold
- ☑ energetic
- ☐ a group
- ☐ married
- ☐ money
- ☐ relaxed
- ☐ time
- ☐ a gym

feel	get	join	spend
energetic			

B Write sentences with *if*. Use some of the words in part A.

1. _If I feel energetic, I might go for a walk._

2. _____

3. _____

4. _____

5. _____

6. _____

7 Complete these sentences with your own information. Add a comma where necessary.

1. If I go shopping on Saturday, I might spend too much money. _____
2. I'll feel healthier _____
   _____
3. If I get more exercise _____
   _____
4. If I don't get good grades in school _____
   _____
5. I might get more sleep _____
   _____
6. I'll be happy _____
   _____

8 Nouns and adjectives

A Complete the chart with another form of the word given.

Noun	Adjective	Noun	Adjective
energy	_____	_____	medical
_____	environmental	success	_____
health	_____		

B Complete the sentences. Use the words in part A.

1. There have been a lot of ___medical___ advances in the past half century, but there is still no cure for the common cold.
2. There are a lot of _____ problems in my country. There's too much air pollution, and the rivers are dirty.
3. My _____ is not as good as it used to be. So, I've decided to eat better food and go swimming every day.
4. My party was a great _____. I think I might have another one soon!
5. If I start exercising more often, I might have more _____.

9 **Rewrite these sentences. Find another way to say each sentence using the words given.**

1. Today, people ride bicycles less often than before. (used to)

   <u>People used to ride bicycles more often than they do today.</u>   OR

   <u>In the past, people used to ride bicycles more often than they do today.</u>

2. If I stop eating junk food, I may be able to lose weight. (diet)

   _____

3. In the future, not many people will use cash to buy things. (few)

   _____

4. If I get a better job, I can buy an apartment. (be able to)

   _____

5. I'm going to arrive at noon. (will)

   _____

10 **Write three paragraphs about yourself. In the first paragraph, describe something about your past. In the second paragraph, write about your life now. In the third paragraph, write about your future.**

> I used to live in a very quiet place ...
>
> Now, I live in a big city. My job is ...
>
> If my English improves, I may be able to get a job with an international company ...
>
> Next year, I'm going to ... I might ...

_____

_____

_____

_____

_____

_____

_____

_____

_____

_____

_____

_____

_____

_____

10 I like working with people.

1 Choose the correct responses.

1. **A:** I enjoy working in sales.

   B: _____

   • Well, I can.   • Neither do I.   • So do I.

2. **A:** I like working the night shift.

   B: _____

   • Well, I don't.   • Neither do I.   • Neither am I.

3. **A:** I can't stand getting to work late.

   B: _____

   • I can't.   • Neither can I.   • Well, I do.

4. **A:** I'm interested in using my language skills.

   B: _____

   • So am I.   • Oh, I don't.   • Oh, I don't mind.

2 Complete the sentences with the words and phrases in the box. Use gerunds.

☐ commute	☐ start her own business	☑ work under pressure
☐ learn languages	☐ use a laptop	☐ work with a team

1. Elena enjoys being a journalist. She has to write a news story by 4:00 P.M. every day, but she doesn't mind _working under pressure_____ .

2. Takiko is a novelist. He writes all his books by hand because he hates _____ .

3. Sarah usually works alone all day, but she enjoys _____ , too.

4. Jennifer works for a large company, but she's interested in _____ .

5. Pablo has to use Portuguese and Japanese at work, but he's not very good at _____ .

6. Annie has to drive to work every day, but she doesn't like _____ .

3 **Rewrite these sentences. Find another way to say each sentence using the words given.**

1. I'm happy to answer the phone. (mind)

  <u>I don't mind answering the phone.</u>

2. I can't make decisions quickly. (not good at)

  _____

3. I hate making mistakes. (stand)

  _____

4. I don't enjoy working alone. (with a team)

  _____

4 **Complete these sentences about yourself. Use gerunds.**

On the job or at school

1. I like <u>meeting people, but I'm a little shy.</u>

2. I can't stand _____

3. I don't mind _____

In my free time

4. I'm interested in _____

5. I'm not interested in _____

At parties or in social situations

6. I'm good at _____

7. I'm not very good at _____

5 **Choose the correct words.**

1. Eric hates waiting in line. He's a very _____ person.
    (impatient / disorganized / punctual)

2. You can trust Marta. If she says she's going to do something, she'll do it.
    She's very _____.
        (hardworking / level-headed / reliable)

3. Kevin isn't good at remembering things. Last week, he missed another
    important business meeting. He's so _____.
                (efficient / forgetful / moody)

6 Job ads on the Internet

A Read these job listings. Match the job titles in the box with the listings below.

_____ flight attendant   _____ journalist   _____ language teacher   _____ stockbroker

JOBSEARCH

find a job

1. Are you hardworking? Do you enjoy using computers? Do you like learning about world news? This job is for you. Must be good at working under pressure. Some evening and weekend work.

2. Must be well organized, energetic, able to make decisions quickly, and good with numbers. Applicants must be level-headed and able to take responsibility for handling other people's money. No weekend work, but some evening work required.

3. No previous experience necessary, but applicant must be willing to work long hours. Successful applicant will also be punctual and reliable. Excellent position for someone who enjoys traveling.

4. Have you studied a foreign language? You may be the right person for this position. Applicants should be comfortable speaking in front of a group and they should be able to communicate well with others.

B What key word(s) in each job ad helped you find the answers in part A?

1. _____
2. _____
3. _____
4. _____

C Which job would be the best for you? The worst? Number them from 1 (the best) to 4 (the worst) and give reasons. List your special experience, preferences, or personal traits.

Job	Reason
_____ language teacher	_____
_____ journalist	_____
_____ flight attendant	_____
_____ stockbroker	_____

7 **Read what these people say about themselves. Then look at the jobs in the box. Choose a job each person should do and a job each person should avoid. Write sentences using *because*.**

☐ accountant	☐ detective	☐ lawyer	☑ nurse	☐ salesperson
☐ carpenter	☐ factory worker	☐ marine biologist	☐ model	☑ social worker

Alan

> I enjoy helping people, but I can't stand working nights and weekends.

1. (make a good / could never) _Alan would probably make a good social worker because he enjoys helping people. He could never be a nurse because he can't stand working nights and weekends._

> I really like doing things with my hands. I also enjoy working with wood. I don't enjoy working in the same place every day, and I hate being in noisy places.

Olivia

2. (could / couldn't) _____
_____

Margo

> I'm really interested in meeting people, and I enjoy wearing different clothes every day. I'm not so good at organizing my time, and I don't like to argue.

3. (would make a good / would make a bad) _____
_____

> I'm really good at selling things. I also love helping people. But I'm not so good at solving problems.

Ha-joon

4. (could be / wouldn't make a good) _____
_____

Eddie

> I love the outdoors and I'm very interested in the sea. I don't like sitting in an office all day, and I'm not good with numbers.

5. (would make a good / wouldn't want to be) _____
_____

8 Add *a* or *an* in the correct places.

1. Mike could never be ^*a*^ nurse or teacher because he is very short-tempered and impatient with people. On the other hand, he's efficient and reliable person. So he would make good bookkeeper or accountant.

2. Scott would make terrible lawyer or executive. He isn't good at making decisions. On the other hand, he'd make excellent actor or artist because he's very creative and funny.

9 Opposites

A Write the opposites. Use the words in the box.

☐ boring	☐ forgetful	☐ late	☐ outgoing
☑ disorganized	☐ impatient	☐ moody	☐ unfriendly

1. efficient / _disorganized_
2. friendly / _____
3. punctual / _____
4. interesting / _____

5. level-headed / _____
6. patient / _____
7. quiet / _____
8. reliable / _____

B Complete the sentences with the words in part A.

1. Mingyu is an _____ person. She really enjoys meeting new people.
2. Hannah is very _____. One day she's happy, and the next day she's sad.
3. I can't stand working with _____ people. I like having reliable co-workers.
4. Charles is an _____ person. I'm never bored when I talk to him.

10 Skills

A Choose the correct word to complete each sentence.

☐ critical	☐ efficient	☐ forgetful	☐ generous
☐ impatient	☐ level-headed	☑ reliable	☐ strict

1. I always do my job well. My boss never has to worry because I'm _____reliable_____.

2. Ed would make a great nurse because he's so _____. He never gets anxious or upset when things go wrong.

3. A good lawyer has to remember facts. Nathan is a terrible lawyer because he's very _____.

4. My favorite teacher at school was Mrs. Wilson. She was pretty _____, so no one misbehaved in her class.

5. My boss is very _____. She gave me a big holiday bonus.

6. June's assistant is very _____. She works fast and never wastes time.

7. My boss complains about everything I do. He's so _____.

8. Julie is so _____. She can't stand waiting for anything.

B Complete the conversations. Use the phrases in the box.

☐ Neither do	☐ Neither am	☐ Neither is	☐ I don't mind
☐ So is	☐ I am	☐ Neither can	☐ So am

1. **A:** I'm not very good at video games. How about you?
   B: Oh, _____. I play video games every weekend.

2. **A:** Jake is not punctual.
   B: _____ Karen. She's always late.

3. **A:** I'm so disorganized!
   B: _____ I. My desk is a mess. I can never find anything.

4. **A:** I don't mind traveling for work.
   B: _____ I. I think it's kind of fun.

5. **A:** I can't stand working in the evening.
   B: _____ I. I prefer to work during the day.

6. **A:** I'm not very outgoing at parties.
   B: _____ I. I'm usually pretty quiet at social events.

7. **A:** I hate taking the train to work.
   B: _____. I usually read or listen to music when I'm on the train.

8. **A:** Stella is really creative.
   B: _____ Robert. He always has great ideas.

11 It's really worth seeing!

1 Complete these sentences. Use the passive form of the verbs in the box.

- ☐ compose
- ☐ discover
- ☐ paint
- ☑ design
- ☐ invent
- ☐ write

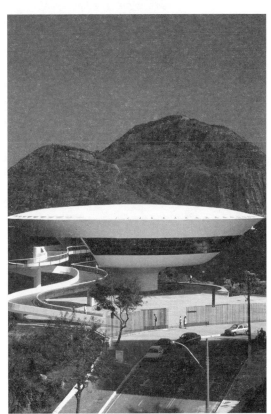

1. The Niterói Contemporary Art Museum in Brazil
   _____was designed_____ by the architect
   Oscar Niemeyer.

2. The play *Romeo and Juliet* _____
   by William Shakespeare in the 1590s.

3. The microwave oven _____
   by Percy Spencer in 1947.

4. The picture *Sunflowers* _____
   by Vincent van Gogh in 1888.

5. In 1960, a 1,000-year-old Viking settlement in Canada
   _____ by Norwegian explorer
   Helge Ingstad.

6. The song "Let It Go" from the movie *Frozen*
   _____ by a married couple,
   Robert Lopez and Kristen Anderson-Lopez.

2 Change these active sentences into the passive.

1. Scientists first identified the Ebola virus in 1976.
   The Ebola virus was first identified by scientists in 1976.

2. J. J. Abrams directed the box-office hit *Star Wars: The Force Awakens*.
   _____

3. The Soviet Union launched the first satellite into space in 1957.
   _____

4. E. B. White wrote the children's novel *Charlotte's Web*.
   _____

5. Frank Lloyd Wright designed the Guggenheim Museum in New York City.
   _____

3 Write sentences. Use the simple past form of the passive with *by*.

1. Angkor Wat

builder: Suryavarman II
year: 1150

2. the Blue Mosque

designer: Mehmet Aga
year: 1616

3. Buckingham Palace

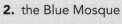

builder: the Duke of Buckingham
year: 1705

4. Canberra, Australia

planner: Walter Burley Griffin
year: 1913

5. the Vasco da Gama Bridge

designer: Armando Rito
year: 1998

6. the Burj Khalifa

builders: 12,000 workers
year: 2010

1. _Angkor Wat was built by Suryavarman II in 1150._ _____

2. _____

3. _____

4. _____

5. _____

6. _____

4 Which city?

A Read about these cities. Write the cities in the box next to the correct descriptions below.

☐ Cusco, Peru ☐ Bogotá, Columbia ☐ Valparaíso, Chile

☐ Rio de Janeiro, Brazil ☐ Montevideo, Uruguay ☐ Ottawa, Canada

_____ This capital city's name is taken from the word *adawa* in the Algonquin language, which probably means "to trade."

_____ The Spanish explorer Juan de Saavedra named this city after his village in Spain. The name means "Valley of Paradise."

_____ The name of this city, which means "River of January" in English, comes from the fact that it was discovered by the Portuguese on January 1, 1502. However, there's no river in the city, just the bay!

_____ The name of this city comes from the expression *Qusqu Wanka* (Owl of the Rock) in Quechua, the language of the Incas. The myth was that a hero who grew wings discovered the place and then became a rock to mark the spot.

_____ The most popular belief about the name of this city is that it comes from the Portuguese expression *monte vid eu* (I saw a hill), spoken by a sailor who first saw this spot in January of 1520.

_____ The name of this city comes from the indigenous Muisca language, but the original word was *bacatá* (planted fields).

B Check (✓) True or False. For statements that are false, write the correct information.

	True	False
1. Both Bogotá and Ottawa were named after a person.	☐	☐
2. Montevideo and Valparaíso were named by explorers.	☐	☐
3. Cusco was named after the mythological story of a bird.	☐	☐
4. Rio de Janeiro was named because of the month of the year it was discovered.	☐	☐

5 Add *is* or *are* where necessary.

Ecuador ˄is˄ situated on the equator in the northwest of South America. It made up of a coastal plain in the west and a tropical rain forest in the east. These two areas separated by the Andes mountains in the center of the country.

The economy based on oil and agricultural products. More oil produced in Ecuador than any other South American country except Venezuela. Bananas, coffee, and cocoa grown there. Many of these products exported. Hardwood also produced and exported.

Many people in Ecuador are of Incan origin. Several native languages spoken there, such as Quechua. Spanish spoken in Ecuador, too.

6 Complete the sentences. Use the words in the box.

| ☑ handicrafts | ☐ electronics | ☐ peso | ☐ wheat |
| ☐ beef | ☐ mining | ☐ tourism | |

1. In many countries, __handicrafts__ are sold by people who make them as well as sell them.
2. The _____ is the currency that is used in Chile.
3. Millions of people visit Italy every year. _____ is a very important industry there.
4. A lot of meat, especially _____, is exported by Argentina.
5. Gold _____ is an important industry in South Africa.
6. Much of the world's _____ is grown in the Canadian prairies. It's used to make foods like bread and pasta.
7. A lot of computers are exported by Taiwan. In fact, the _____ industry is an important part of many East Asian economies.

7 Complete this paragraph with *is* or *are* and the past participle of the verbs in the box. Some words may be used more than once.

border	divide	find	locate
call	fill	know	visit

Every year, millions of tourists visit California. California _____ for its beautiful scenery, warm climate, and excellent food. There are many national parks in California. They _____ by over 30 million people every year. Many world-famous museums _____ there, including the Getty Center in Los Angeles and the San Francisco Museum of Modern Art.

The state _____ into two parts, called Northern California and Southern California. San Francisco and Yosemite National Park _____ in Northern California.

San Francisco _____ by water on three sides. It is a city with a beautiful bay and two famous bridges. San Francisco's streets _____ always _____ with tourists. On the north end of the bay is the world-famous Napa Valley. South of San Francisco, there is an area that is famous for its computer industries; it _____ Silicon Valley. Many computer industries _____ there. Los Angeles, Hollywood, and Disneyland _____ in Southern California. Southern California _____ for its desert areas, which are sometimes next to snowcapped mountains.

8 Rewrite these sentences. Find another way to say each sentence using the words given.

1. The designer of the Montjuic Tower in Barcelona was Santiago Calatrava. (designed)

    _____

2. Switzerland has four official languages. (spoken)

    _____

3. In South Korea, a lot of people work in the automobile industry. (employed)

    _____

4. Malaysia has a prime minister. (governed)

    _____

9 Wh- questions and indirect questions

A Look at the answers. Write Wh- questions.

1. What _____

   The telephone was invented by Alexander Graham Bell.

2. Where _____

   Acapulco is located in southern Mexico.

3. When _____

   Santiago, Chile, was founded in 1541.

4. What _____

   Rice is grown in Thailand.

B Look at the answers. Write indirect questions.

1. Do you know _____

   The Golden Gate Bridge is located in San Francisco.

2. Can you tell me _____

   Don Quixote was written by Miguel de Cervantes.

3. Do you know _____

   Antibiotics were first used in 1941.

4. Could you tell me _____

   The tea bag was invented by Thomas Sullivan in 1908.

10 Complete the sentences. Use the passive of the words given.

1804	The first steam locomotive _____ was built _____ (build) in Britain.
1829	A speed record of 58 kph (36 mph) _____ (establish) by a train in Britain.
1863	The world's first underground railway _____ (open) in London.
1964	"Bullet train" service _____ (introduce) in Japan.
1990	A speed of 512 kph (320 mph) _____ (reach) by a French high-speed train.
1995	Maglevs _____ (test) in several countries. These trains use magnets to lift them above the ground.
2006	The Qinghai-Tibet railway _____ (finish). It is the world's highest railway and reaches 5,072 meters (16,640 feet).
2011	The journey time from Beijing to Shanghai _____ (reduce) from 10 hours to 5.5 hours by the new maglev train.

12 It's a long story.

1 Describe what these people were doing when a fire alarm went off in their apartment building last night. Use the past continuous.

1 Carolyn	2 Peter	3 the Mitchells
4 Isabella and Carlos	5 Mr. Yang	6 Paula

1. <u>Carolyn was washing the dishes when the fire alarm went off.</u>
2. _____
3. _____
4. _____
5. _____
6. _____

2 Describe your activities yesterday. What were you doing at these times?

At 9:00 A.M.

At 9:00 A.M., I was having
breakfast at a coffee shop
with my friends.

About 10:00 last night

_____

_____

_____

In the afternoon

_____

_____

_____

Around noon

_____

_____

_____

At 11:00 in the morning

_____

_____

_____

At this time yesterday

_____

_____

_____

3 Complete the conversation with the correct word or phrase.

Matt: How did you get your first job, Sonia?

Sonia: Well, I _____*got*_____ a summer job in a department store
(got / was getting)

while I _____ at the university.
(studied / was studying)

Matt: No, I mean your first full-time job.

Sonia: But that *is* how I got my first full-time job. I _____ during the
(worked / was working)

summer when the manager _____ me a job after graduation.
(offered / was offering)

Matt: Wow! That was lucky. Did you like the job?

Sonia: Well, I did at first, but then things changed. I _____ the same
(did / was doing)

thing every day, and they _____ me any new responsibilities.
(didn't give / weren't giving)

I _____ really bored when another company
(got / was getting)

_____ me to work for them.
(asked / was asking)

4 Look at the pictures and complete these sentences.

1. My roommate was studying when
   _she fell asleep!_____

2. I saw an old friend last week while
   _____

3. My car was giving me a lot of trouble, so
   _____

4. Coffee arrived while
   _____

5   One foot in one country, one foot in another

A   Scan the article. Why is Lila Downs famous?

Lila Downs

Lila Downs is a Grammy-award winning singer and songwriter who is famous not only in Mexico and the United States, but throughout the world.

Lila was born in the state of Oaxaca, Mexico in 1968. Her mother belongs to the indigenous Mixtec people who speak both Mixtec and Spanish. Her father, who died when Lila was sixteen, was a professor of art and film from the United States. As a girl living in and traveling between Mexico and the U.S., Lila picked up the musical influences that give her music a very international flavor. She still travels a lot between Mexico and the U.S. because her husband is from Minnesota.

Lila is trilingual. She sings in Mixtec, Spanish, and English. She can sing in other languages, too. She learned to sing as a child by listening to her mother, who was a professional singer of Mexican popular music. Lila's first big success came in 1999 with her album *La Sandunga*, which is the name of a traditional dance in Oaxaca. In 2005 she went on to win the Latin Grammy award for *Una Sangre (One Blood)*.

Lila became known to many people through her singing performance in *Frida*, the 2002 film about the famous Mexican artist Frida Kahlo. She has acted in and contributed music to a number of films, while also writing the music and lyrics with her husband to the musical version of *Como agua para chocolate (Like Water for Chocolate)*, based on the very popular book by Mexican novelist Laura Esquivel.

Although she studied classical voice at college in the United States, Lila has devoted a great part of her career to singing the music of Mexico in Spanish, Mixtec, and Zapotec, which is another indigenous language in the state of Mexico. Many of her songs are concerned with social justice.

B   Read the article and check (✓) True or False. For statements that are false, write the correct information.

	True	False
1. Lila Downs' father was a professor of literature in the United States.	☐	☐
2. Her husband is from the United States.	☐	☐
3. She wrote the book *Como agua para chocolate*.	☐	☐
4. She studied classical voice in college in Mexico.	☐	☐
5. She speaks Spanish, Mixtec, and English.	☐	☐

6 How long has it been?

A Write sentences. Use the present perfect continuous and *for* or *since*.

> **Grammar note: *for* and *since***
>
> **Use *for* to describe a period of time.**
> *Linda has been living in Seattle **for three months**.*
> *I haven't been jogging **for very long**.*
> **Use *since* to describe a point of time in the past.**
> *Linda has been living in Seattle **since she changed jobs**.*
> *I haven't been jogging **since I hurt my foot**.*

1. Annie / work / actor / three years

    Annie has been working as an actor for three years.

2. Carrie and Alex / go / graduate school / August

    _____

3. Tom / study / Chinese / a year

    _____

4. Linda / not teach / she had a baby

    _____

5. Lori / not live / Los Angeles / very long

    _____

6. Luis and Silvina / travel / South America / six weeks

    _____

B Write sentences about yourself. Use the phrases and clauses in the box (or your own information) and *for* or *since*.

18 months	a few weeks
2006	I was in high school
ages	this morning

1. I haven't been swimming in ages. _____
2. _____
3. _____
4. _____
5. _____
6. _____

7 Look at the answers. Write the questions.

Mark: <u>What have you been doing lately?</u>

Andrew: I've been working a lot and trying to stay in shape.

Mark: _____

Andrew: No, I haven't been jogging. I've been playing tennis in the evenings with friends.

Mark: Really? _____

Andrew: No, I've been losing most of the games. But it's fun. How about you?
_____

Mark: No, I haven't been getting any exercise. I've been working long hours every day.

Andrew: _____

Mark: Yes, I've even been working on weekends. I've been working Saturday mornings.

Andrew: Well, why don't we play a game of tennis on Saturday afternoon? It's great exercise!

8 Choose the correct responses.

1. A: When I was a kid, I lived on a farm.

   B: _____

- Really? Tell me more.
- Oh, have you?
- So have I.

2. A: I haven't been ice-skating in ages.

   B: _____

- Why were you?
- Wow! I have, too.
- Neither have I.

3. A: I was a teenager when I got my first job.

   B: _____

- Really? Where do you work?
- Really? That's interesting.
- For five years.

4. A: I haven't seen you for a long time.

   B: _____

- I didn't know that.
- Not since we graduated.
- Hmm, I have no idea.

9 Complete the answers to the questions. Use the past continuous or the present perfect continuous of the verbs given.

1. **A:** Have you been working here for long?

   B: No, I _haven't been working_ (work) here for very long –
   only since January.

2. **A:** Were you living in Europe before you moved here?

   B: No, I _____ (live) in South Korea.

3. **A:** How long have you been studying English?

   B: I _____ (study) it for about a year.

4. **A:** What were you doing before you went back to school?

   B: I _____ (sell) real estate.

5. **A:** What have you been doing since I last saw you?

   B: I _____ (travel) around the country.

10 Rewrite these sentences. Find another way to say each sentence using the words given.

1. Terri was about 15 when she started saving up for a world trip. (teenager)

   Terri started saving up for a world trip
   while she was a teenager.

2. I was getting dressed when my friend arrived. (while)

   _____

   _____

3. I've been a fan of that TV show since I was a kid. (a long time)

   _____

   _____

4. I've had a part-time job for a year. (last year)

   _____

   _____

5. I've been spending too much money lately. (not save enough)

   _____

   _____

6. I haven't seen you for a long time. (ages)

   _____

   _____

13 That's entertainment!

1 **Choose the correct words to complete these movie reviews.**

Classic Movie Review

Login / Register

Home   Reviews   News   Archives   Search

Indiana Jones and the Kingdom of the Crystal Skull

This action movie is dumb. It has

____amazing____ (amazed / amazing)

action scenes, but the story is really

_____ (bored / boring). I think

the other Indiana Jones movies were

_____ (excited / exciting), but

I think this one is ridiculous.

Brian's Song

This drama is based on a _____

(fascinated / fascinating) true story. It's about Brian

Piccolo, a football player who develops a terrible

disease, and his friend Gayle Sayers. Maybe

it doesn't sound _____ (interested /

interesting), but it's a must-see. The film has

great acting and a wonderful script. I was very

_____ (moved / moving) by the story of

the friendship between Piccolo and Sayers.

2 **Choose the correct words.**

1. Denzel Washington was __outstanding__ (horrible / ridiculous / outstanding) in his last movie. I think he's a really great actor.

2. I really enjoyed all of the *Hunger Games* movies. In fact, I think they're _____ (terrible / wonderful / boring).

3. The special effects were great in that sci-fi movie we saw last week. They can do such _____ (silly / dumb / incredible) things with 3-D technology these days.

4. The latest *Star Wars* movie was _____ (dumb / disgusting / fantastic), and I'd love to see it again.

3 Choose the correct responses.

1. A: I think that Keira Knightly is very pretty.

    B: _Oh, I do, too._

      • Oh, I do, too.

      • I don't like her either.

2. A: His new movie is the dumbest movie I've ever seen.

    B: _____

      • Yeah, I liked it, too.

      • I didn't like it either.

3. A: It's weird that they don't show more classic movies on TV. I really like them.

    B: _____

      • I know. It's really wonderful.

      • I know. It's strange.

4. A: I think Tina Fey is hilarious.

    B: _____

      • Yeah, she's horrible.

      • Yeah, she's excellent.

5. A: The movie we saw last night was ridiculous.

    B: _____

      • Yes, I agree. It was exciting.

      • Well, I thought it was pretty good.

4 Write two sentences for each of these categories.

1. Things you think are exciting

    I think paragliding is exciting.

    _____

2. Things you are interested in

    _____

    _____

3. Things you think are boring

    _____

    _____

4. Things you are disgusted by

    _____

    _____

5 Movie classics on the Internet

A Read about these movies available online. Write the number of the movie next to its type.

_____ fantasy   _____ war movie   _____ romantic drama   _____ science fiction

Movie Classics

1. *Casablanca* (1945)

This is the story of two people in love during World War II who are waiting in Casablanca for a chance to escape from the war. Starring Humphrey Bogart and Ingmar Bergman and directed by John Huston, this movie is a must!

2. *Pan's Labyrinth* (2006)

This movie blends a story of the Spanish Civil War with the mythological fantasies of a young girl (Ivana Baquero). It takes place in the mountains of northern Spain where legends of strange creatures are still told. The movie was written and directed by Guillermo de Toro. It is a masterpiece and it is out of this world!

3. *2001: A Space Odyssey* (1968)

Directed by Stanley Kubrick, this is a story about two astronauts who are on a fatal mission in outer space. But it's the ship's computer, HAL, who really steals the show.

4. *The Bridge Over the River Kwai* (1957)

You will never forget the music of this film! And you will understand why many people think it is one of the best movies ever made about war. It is the story of British and American soldiers who are prisoners of war. They must build a bridge in Burma during World War II. You will not be disappointed!

B Write the name of the movie described.

1. a movie with an unusual "star": _____

2. two lovers in a difficult situation: _____

3. where dreams and reality meet: _____

4. its music is unforgettable: _____

C Match the expressions in column A with their meanings in column B.

A	B
1. you won't be disappointed _____	**a.** you need to see it
2. out of this world _____	**b.** becomes the center of attention
3. it's a must _____	**c.** you're going to like it
4. steals the show _____	**d.** outstanding

6 Tell me more!

A Rewrite these sentences. Use *who* or *which*.

1. *The Sound of Music* is a movie. It has been very popular for a long time.

   The Sound of Music is a movie which has been very popular for a long time.

2. *The Theory of Everything* is a movie. It is based on a true story about Stephen Hawking.

   _____

3. Elizabeth Taylor was an actress. She won two Academy Awards.

   _____

4. Akira Kurosawa was a director. He was one of the most influential filmmakers in history.

   _____

5. *The Miracle Worker* is a great movie. It won a lot of awards.

   _____

6. Jennifer Lopez is an actress, a dancer, and a singer. She also appears on TV.

   _____

B Write two sentences like those in part A about movies and entertainers. Use *who* or *which*.

1. _____
2. _____

7 Complete the sentences. Use *that* for things or *who* for people.

Heather: Who is Mark Twain?

Carlos: Oh, you know him. He's an author _____who_____ wrote a lot of novels about life in America in the 1800s.

Heather: Oh, I remember. He wrote several stories _____ people have to read in literature classes, right?

Carlos: Yes, but people love reading them for pleasure, too.

Heather: What's his most popular book?

Carlos: I guess *Adventures of Huckleberry Finn* is the one _____ is most famous. It's a work _____ has been very popular since it was published in 1885.

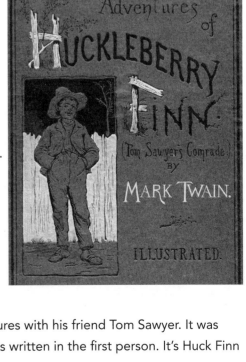

Heather: Ah, yes, I think I've heard of it. What's it about?

Carlos: It's about a boy _____ has a lot of adventures with his friend Tom Sawyer. It was one of the first American novels _____ was written in the first person. It's Huck Finn himself _____ tells the story.

Heather: Now, that's a story _____ I'd like to read.

8 Different kinds of movies

A Write definitions for these different kinds of movies. Use relative clauses and the phrases in the box.

☐	has a love story
✓	has cowboys in it
☐	has a lot of excitement
☐	is about a real person
☐	is scary
☐	makes you laugh
☐	shows real events

1. A western _is a movie that has cowboys in it._
2. A romance _____
3. A comedy _____
4. An action film _____
5. A horror film _____
6. A biography _____
7. A documentary _____

B What kind of movie in part A is your favorite? Your least favorite?
Write one paragraph about each and give reasons for your opinions.

My Favorite Kind of Movie

I really like action movies. They are movies that make me forget about all my problems. . . .

_____
_____
_____
_____
_____

My Least Favorite Kind of Movie

I don't like horror movies because I think they are really dumb. Usually, the story has characters
who are not very scary. . . .

_____
_____
_____
_____
_____

9 Complete these sentences. Use the words in the box.

- ☐ character
- ☐ cinematography
- ☐ composer
- ☐ special effects

1. I thought the _____ in the *Jurassic Park* movies were cool. It's incredible what they can do with computers.

2. Have you ever seen the 1965 film *Doctor Zhivago*? The _____ is beautiful, especially the lighting.

3. Hermione Granger is my favorite _____ in the *Harry Potter* books.

4. I've forgotten the name of the _____ who wrote *Rhapsody in Blue*. Was it George Gershwin?

10 Rewrite this movie review. Where possible, join sentences with *who*, *that*, or *which*.

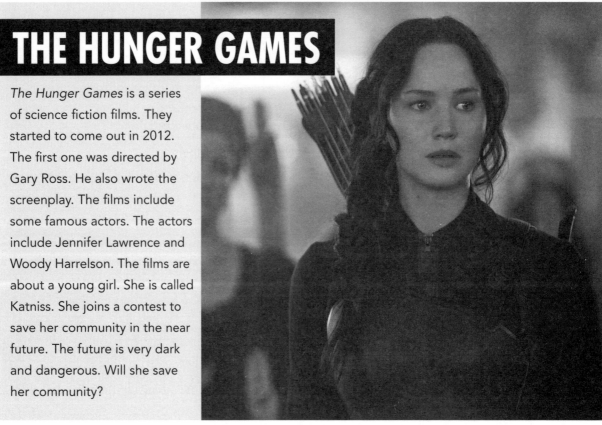

THE HUNGER GAMES

The Hunger Games is a series of science fiction films. They started to come out in 2012. The first one was directed by Gary Ross. He also wrote the screenplay. The films include some famous actors. The actors include Jennifer Lawrence and Woody Harrelson. The films are about a young girl. She is called Katniss. She joins a contest to save her community in the near future. The future is very dark and dangerous. Will she save her community?

The Hunger Games is a series of science fiction films that started to come out in 2012.

_____

_____

_____

_____

_____

14 Now I get it!

1 What does that mean?

A What do these gestures mean? Match the phrases in the box with the gestures.

a. Stop!
b. I want to turn.
c. We need a taxi.
d. We need help.
e. I'm angry!

1. _e_
2. ___
3. ___
4. ___
5. ___

B Write a sentence about each situation in part A using the phrases in the box.

It could mean . . .	It might mean . . .	It must mean . . .
Maybe it means . . .	Perhaps it means . . .	It probably means . . .

1. _It must mean he's angry._
2. _____
3. _____
4. _____
5. _____

2 **Complete the sentences. Use the correct form of the words in the box.**

☐ annoy ☐ confuse ☐ embarrass ☐ frustrate
☐ bore ✓ disgust ☐ exhaust

1. The food in that restaurant is __disgusting__.
   I'll never eat there again!

2. That sign is really _____.
   What does it mean? It's not clear at all.

3. I got stuck behind a really slow bus on a
   narrow mountain road. I felt
   _____ because I couldn't
   pass it.

4. I drove for eight hours on a straight, flat road
   where the scenery never changed. I've never
   been so _____!

5. I couldn't get into the parking space,
   and everyone was looking at me. It was
   pretty _____.

6. I went bicycling all day. Now I'm so
   _____ that I'm going to sleep
   for 12 hours!

7. I asked the taxi driver to turn off his radio
   because the loud music was very
   _____.

3 **What would you say in each situation? Use the sentences in the box.**

☐ Come here. ☐ Shh. Be quiet!
☐ That sounds crazy! ☐ Where's the restroom?

1. Your friend wants to dye his hair green and wear orange contact lenses.
   _____

2. You can't concentrate on the movie because the people in front of you are talking.
   _____

3. You wave to your friend because you want to show her something interesting.
   _____

4. You just ordered a meal and want to wash your hands before you eat.
   _____

4 Proverbs

A Match the proverbs with their meanings.

Proverbs

1. The grass is always greener on the other side of the fence.

2. An ounce of prevention is worth a pound of cure.

3. An apple a day keeps the doctor away.

4. There are plenty of fish in the sea.

5. Better late than never.

6. Birds of a feather flock together.

Meanings

_____ If you eat the right food you will be healthy.

_____ People with the same interests become friends.

__1__ We may think we will be happier in a different situation, but it is not necessarily true.

_____ Don't worry if you love someone who doesn't return your love. You can always find someone else.

_____ It is easier to fix something before there is a problem than after the problem has occurred.

_____ It is preferable to do something with some delay than to never do it at all.

B What would you say? Choose a proverb for each situation.

1. A: I really don't understand what Miriam sees in Bill.

   B: Oh, I do. They both love movies from other countries and they like learning languages.

   A: Ah, I see! _____

2. A: It's 10 o'clock already! Do you think I can get to the party on time?

   B: That depends on whether you can catch the bus.

   A: But what if I don't?

   B: Well, getting there is the important thing. _____

3. A: A penny for your thoughts.

   B: I was just thinking about what it's like to be a movie star.

   A: Do you think they're any happier than you are?

   B: They must be, don't you think?

   A: Oh, I don't know. _____

4. A: It's cold outside. Why don't you put on your new coat?

   B: Do you think I need to, dear?

   A: Well, you don't want to catch a cold like the one you had last month, do you?

   B: OK, you're right. Like they say, _____

5 | What do you think these proverbs mean?

1. Don't cry over spilled milk.

It could mean _____

2. Don't judge a book by its cover.

Maybe it means _____

3. There's no such thing as a free lunch.

It might mean _____

4. Bad news travels fast.

It probably means _____

6 | Complete the conversation. Use each phrase in the box only once.

☐ it might be
☐ it's definitely
☐ you can
☐ you have to
☑ you're not allowed to

Teacher: OK, class. This afternoon, we're going to take the school bus to the science museum.

Student 1: Great! I'm going to take some photos.

Teacher: I'm afraid _you're not allowed to_ take photos.

Student 1: But how can they stop me? I'll use my cell phone, not a camera.

Teacher: _____ check all your things with security.

Student 2: Can I take my jacket into the museum?

Teacher: I'm not sure. _____ best to leave it on the bus.

Student 2: But what about my wallet? It might not be safe on the bus.

Teacher: Oh, _____ a good idea to keep your money with you.
Keep it in your pocket.

Student 3: And what about touching things in the museum?

Teacher: There are "Don't touch!" signs next to some of the things.
But _____ touch things if there is no sign.

7 Look at the numbered photos of signs below. Then complete the conversations between a driving instructor and his student. Use each word or phrase in the box only once.

☐ are allowed to	☐ can	☐ don't have to
☑ aren't allowed to	☐ can't	☐ have to

1. **Student:** This is great!

   Instructor: Hey, slow down! You _aren't allowed to_ go above the speed limit.

2. **Student:** Uh, what does that sign mean?

   Instructor: It means you _____ turn left.

3. **Instructor:** You look confused.

   Student: What . . . what does that sign mean?

   Instructor: It means you _____ do two things. You _____ turn right or go straight.

4. **Instructor:** Why are you stopping?

   Student: The sign says to stop.

   Instructor: Actually, you _____ stop. Just be prepared to, if necessary.

5. **Instructor:** Hey, stop! Didn't you see that sign? It means you _____ come to a complete stop.

   Student: What sign? I didn't see any sign.

8 **Rewrite these sentences. Find another way to say each sentence using the words given.**

1. Maybe it means you're not allowed to fish here. (may)

   It may mean you're not allowed to fish here.

2. You can't light a fire here. (allowed)

   _____

3. Perhaps that sign means you're not allowed to swim here. (might)

   _____

4. I think that sign means you can get food here. (probably)

   _____

5. You need to be quiet after 10:00 P.M. (have got to)

   _____

9 **Complete each conversation using the words in the box.**

☐ confusing ☐ embarrassing ☐ exhausting ☐ impatient ☐ irritating

1. **A:** I went to the movies last night. A couple who sat behind me talked during the entire movie.

   B: That's _____!

2. **A:** I fell asleep during class this afternoon. The teacher had to wake me up.

   B: Oh, that's _____!

3. **A:** I drove all night to get there on time.

   B: Oh, that's _____! How can you keep your eyes open?

4. **A:** Did Sara give you directions to the party?

   B: She did, but they're really _____. Hey, can I get a ride with you?

5. **A:** This movie is taking forever to download. Why does it have to take so long?

   B: You are so _____! There, look. It's done!

15 I wouldn't have done that.

1 I think I'd . . .

A What would you do in these situations? Check (✓) an answer or write your own suggestion.

1. Your classmate leaves her new smartphone in the classroom.

☐ run after her and give it back to her immediately

☐ take it home overnight to try it out

☐ _____

2. Someone climbs through your neighbor's window.

☐ call the police

☐ ring the doorbell

☐ _____

3. Your boss makes things difficult for you at work.

☐ talk to your boss

☐ look for another job

☐ _____

4. A friend sounds unhappy on the phone.

☐ ask your friend if he or she has a problem

☐ tell jokes to make your friend laugh

☐ _____

B Write about what you would do in the situations in part A. Use the phrases in the box.

I'd . . .	I might . . .	I guess I'd . . .
I'd probably . . .	I think I'd . . .	

1. <u>If my classmate left her new smartphone in the classroom,</u>
<u>I think I'd run after her and give it back to her immediately.</u>

2. _____

_____

3. _____

_____

4. _____

_____

2 Complete these sentences with information about yourself.

1. If a relative asked to borrow some money, I'd _____

2. If I had three wishes, _____

3. If I could have any job I wanted, _____

4. If I had a year of vacation time, _____

5. If I could change one thing about myself, _____

3 Choose the correct word.

1. I'd go ___straight___ to the police if I saw someone breaking into a house.
   (seriously / simply / straight)

2. My friend _____ to cheating on the biology exam, but his teacher still failed him.
   (returned / confessed / said)

3. I'm in a difficult _____ at work. I don't know whether to talk to my boss about it or just quit.
   (divorce / predicament / problem)

4. If I saw someone _____ in a store, I'd tell the store manager immediately.
   (cheating / shoplifting / shopping)

5. My uncle died and left me $20,000. I'm going to _____ most of it.
   (invest / return / sell)

6. When I went back to the parking lot, I tried to get into someone else's car _____ mistake.
   (by / in / with)

7. There is so much great music to download from the Internet. I don't know what to _____.
   (choose / confess / fix)

8. My aunt won't let me use her car because she thinks I'm a terrible driver.
   She has a _____. I had two accidents last year!
   (flat tire / point / reward)

4 What to do?

A Read the article. Match what happened to a possible action.

What happened

1. You bought a camera on sale at a store, but it didn't work right. The salesclerk said, "We can't do anything about it."

2. You checked your bank statement and noticed that there was a deposit of $1,000. You didn't make the deposit. You're sure it was a bank error.

3. You sat on a park bench that had wet paint on it. You ruined your clothes. There was no "Wet Paint" sign.

4. You were not happy with the grade you got in an important class.

5. Your next-door neighbors borrowed your vacuum cleaner. When they returned it, it was damaged.

6. A friend gave you an expensive vase for your birthday, but you didn't really like it.

Possible actions

_____ I guess I'd take it back to the store and exchange it for something else.

_____ I guess I'd write a letter of complaint to the manufacturer.

_____ Maybe I'd ask them to repair it.

_____ I think I'd make an appointment to see the instructor to talk about it.

_____ I'd probably wait until the next month to see if the mistake is corrected.

_____ I'd write a letter to the city council and ask them to pay for the damage.

B What would you do in each situation? Write another possible action.

1. _____

2. _____

3. _____

4. _____

5. _____

6. _____

5 What would you have done in these situations? Use *would have* or *wouldn't have*.

1. Lisa had dinner in a restaurant and then realized she didn't have any money. She offered to wash the dishes.

I wouldn't have washed the dishes. I would have
called a friend to bring me some money.

2. Alex was on a bus when the woman next to him started talking loudly on a cell phone. He asked her to speak more quietly.

_____

_____

3. Ryan invited two friends to dinner on Friday, but they came on Thursday by mistake. He told them to come back the next day.

_____

_____

4. Luke's neighbors had their TV on very loud late at night. Luke called and complained to the police.

_____

_____

5. Sharon had a houseguest who was supposed to stay for three days, but the woman was still there three weeks later. Sharon finally gave her a bill for her room and board.

_____

_____

6. Margo accidentally broke a glass at a friend's house. She decided not to say anything about it.

_____

_____

6 Write two things you should have done or shouldn't have done last week, last month, and last year.

1. Last week: _Last week, I should have . . ._ _____

_____

2. Last month: _____

_____

3. Last year: _____

_____

7 Advice column

A Complete each letter with the correct forms of the verbs in each box.

☐ borrow	☐ disagree	☑ marry	☐ spend
☐ deny	☐ enjoy	☐ save	☐ lose

● ● ● < >   🔍 🏠

✉ Ask Harriet

Dear Harriet,

I've never written to an advice columnist before, but I have a big problem. I'm going out with this really nice guy. He's very sweet to me, and I really want to ____marry____ him. In fact, we plan to have our wedding next summer. But he has a problem with money. He _____ money like crazy! Sometimes he _____ money from me, but he never pays it back. I want to _____ money because I want us to buy an apartment when we get married. However, if I tell him he has a problem with money, he _____ it. He says, "I _____ with you. You never want to go out and _____ yourself." I don't want to _____ him, but what can I do? – J. M., Seattle

☐ accept	☐ admit	☑ agree
☐ find	☐ forget	☐ refuse

● ● ● < >   🔍 🏠

Dear J. M.,

You and your boyfriend must ____agree____ on how you spend your money *before* you get married. If you both _____ that there is a problem, you could probably _____ an answer. He should _____ your idea of saving some money. And you shouldn't always _____ to go out and have fun. Don't _____ that talking can really help.

Good luck! – Harriet

B What advice would you give J. M.? Write a reply to her letter.

_____

_____

_____

_____

_____

_____

8 To accept or to refuse?

A Complete the conversation with *would* or *should* and the correct tense of the verbs given.

Carly: Guess what, Kristin! A university in New Zealand has offered me a scholarship.

Kristin: Great! When are you going?

Carly: That's just it. I may not go. What _____would_____ you _____do_____ (do) if your boyfriend asked you not to go?

Kristin: Well, I _____ (try) to convince him that it's a good opportunity for me.

Carly: I've tried that. He said I could study the same thing here.

Kristin: If I were you, I _____ (talk) to him again. You know, I once missed a big opportunity.

Carly: Oh? What happened?

Kristin: I was offered a job in Los Angeles, but my husband disliked the idea of moving, so we didn't go. I _____ (take) the job. I've always regretted my decision. In my situation, what _____ you _____ (do)?

Carly: Oh, I _____ (accept) the offer.

Kristin: Well, there's the answer to your predicament. Accept the scholarship!

B What would you do if you were Carly? Why?

If I were Carly, . . . _____

_____

9 What would you do if you found a diamond ring? Complete these sentences.

1. I would _hide it and come back for it later._
2. I wouldn't _____
3. I could _____
4. I might _____
5. I might not _____

16 Making excuses

1 **People are making many requests of Eric. Write the requests.**
Use *ask*, *tell*, or *say* and reported speech.

1.	**Mark:**	"Eric, take my phone calls."
2.	**Julie:**	"Can you do an Internet search for me, Eric?"
3.	**Andrew:**	"Could you check this flash drive for viruses?"
4.	**Tanya:**	"Eric, put this information on a spreadsheet."
5.	**Carla:**	"Don't forget to add paper to the copier, Eric."
6.	**Alan:**	"Reformat this text file as a PDF file."
7.	**Bruce:**	"Get me some coffee, Eric."
8.	**Cindy:**	"Make five copies of the agenda before the meeting."
9.	**Jack:**	"Could you give me a ride home?"
10.	**Robin:**	"Don't be late to work again."

1. Mark told Eric to take his phone calls.

2. _____

3. _____

4. _____

5. _____

6. _____

7. _____

8. _____

9. _____

10. _____

2 Nouns and verbs

A Complete the chart.

Noun	Verb	Noun	Verb
acceptance	accept	_____	explain
_____	apologize	_____	invite
_____	complain	_____	offer
_____	excuse	_____	suggest

B Complete these sentences. Use the correct form of the words from part A.

1. This coffee tastes awful. I'm going to __complain__ to the waiter about it.

2. I _____ an invitation to Billy and Kate's house for dinner.

3. I didn't want to go to Jenny's party, so I made up an _____.

4. I was rude to my teacher. I must _____ to him.

5. Can you _____ the end of the movie? I didn't understand it.

6. Steve said he'd take me to the airport. It was really nice of him to _____.

7. Thank you for your helpful _____ on how to fix my essay. The teacher really liked it!

8. I received an _____ to Mindy's party. I can't wait to go.

3 Choose the correct verb. Use the past tense.

☐ express   ☐ give   ☐ make   ☑ offer   ☐ tell

1. Jennifer told me she was graduating from college, so I __offered__ her my congratulations.

2. I _____ a complaint to the police because our neighbors' party was too noisy.

3. I couldn't go to the meeting, so I _____ my concerns in an email.

4. Jake _____ an excuse for being late for work. He said there had been a traffic jam on the highway.

5. Lori was very funny at the class party. As usual, she _____ a lot of jokes.

4 What a great excuse!

A Read the invitations and excuses in these text messages between Eileen and William. Underline the phrases that are invitations or excuses.

Hi, William. It would be wonderful if you could come to our party next Friday! It's Mick's birthday and I really think that he would appreciate it if you could be there. All of his friends will be there. The best part is that Mick doesn't know everyone is going to be there. It's a surprise birthday party! So please come and be part of the surprise.

Hi, Eileen. Thank you for the invitation. You know I would love to come if I could, but unfortunately I am working late on Friday. I have to study for my examination next week. So, have a great time without me, and of course I will send a present to Mick.

Oh, William, come on! Please come. The best present you can give to Mick is being with him on his birthday. I know everyone would really enjoy seeing you, too.

Eileen, I really should study for the test. I know I will probably regret not going, but I think I should stick to my plan.

William, you are so right when you say you will regret it if you don't come to Mick's birthday party. All of your friends will be there. As a matter of fact, I mentioned you to Penelope and she said she is looking forward to talking to you at the party. We will all be disappointed if you don't come. Especially Penelope!

Eileen, I've given it some thought and you are right! I should go to Mick's party. In fact, wild horses couldn't stop me. See you on Friday!

B Read the phrases that you underlined. Answer these questions.

1. Why did Eileen text William?

2. Why can't William come to the party?

3. Why do you think William decided to accept the invitation after all?

5 Sorry, but . . .

A The teacher wants to have a class picnic on Saturday. Look at the excuses that students gave her. Change each excuse into reported speech using *say*.

1. Tim: "I'm getting my hair cut."

   Tim said he was getting his hair cut.

2. Teresa: "My sister is having a baby shower."

   _____

3. Bill: "I may have some houseguests on Saturday."

   _____

4. Miyako and Yoshiko: "We're going camping this weekend."

   _____

5. Marco: "I'm sorry, but I'll be busy on Saturday afternoon."

   _____

B Change these excuses into reported speech using *tell*.

1. Abbie: "I signed up for a scuba diving class."

   Abbie told her she had signed up for a scuba diving class.

2. Paul and James: "We'll be moving to our new apartment that day."

   _____

3. Luis: "I watch the football game on TV every Saturday."

   _____

4. Sandra: "I've already made plans to do something else."

   _____

C Write excuses for three more students. Use your own ideas.

1. _____

2. _____

3. _____

6 What did they say?

A Match the reports of what people said in column A with the descriptions in column B.

A	B
1. Sam said that he was talking to Jim in the office for an hour. He's very unhappy about the new company rules. __c__	**a.** giving a reason
2. Brian said that the game was canceled because of bad weather. _____	**b.** refusing an invitation
3. Nina said she would be studying on Saturday night. (But she'll actually be at the movies.) _____	**c.** making a complaint
4. Carl told me he couldn't come for dinner on Friday. He said he had to work late. _____	**d.** telling a lie
5. Max told me that he didn't want to go to the party because Kayla would be there. _____	**e.** making an excuse

B Write each person's original words.

1. Sam: _"I was talking to Jim in the office for an hour. He's very unhappy about the new company rules."_

2. Brian: _____

_____

3. Nina: _____

_____

4. Carl: _____

_____

5. Max: _____

_____

7 Choose the correct responses.

1. **A:** We're going to go hiking. Do you want to join us?

   B: _____

   • Sorry, I won't be able to.   • What's up?

2. **A:** I'm really sorry. We'll be out of town this weekend.

   B: _____

   • I've made other plans.   • No problem.

3. **A:** Meet us at 7:00. OK?

   B: _____

   • Oh, that's all right.   • OK, sounds like fun.

4. **A:** I'm sorry. I won't be able to make it.

   B: _____

   • Well, never mind.   • Great.

8 Yes or no?

A Which expressions would you use to accept an invitation? To refuse an invitation?
Check (✓) the correct answer.

	Accept	Refuse
1. I'm really sorry.	☐	☐
2. Great.	☐	☐
3. Sounds like fun.	☐	☐
4. I've made other plans.	☐	☐
5. I won't be able to make it.	☐	☐
6. I'm busy.	☐	☐
7. Thanks a lot.	☐	☐
8. I'd love to.	☐	☐

B Use the expressions in part A to accept or refuse these invitations. Offer an excuse if you refuse.

1. Would you like to come to a soccer match with me tomorrow?

   _____

2. That new action movie looks great! Do you want to see it with me?

   _____

3. A friend asked me to go to the mall after class. Do you want to join us?

   _____